Worship God Again

Enter His Presence
Like It's Your First Time

Dr. Mark A. Bethel

Enter His Presence
Like It's Your First Time

ISBN: 978-0-9847460-7-1
ISBN: 978-0-9847460-8-8 (Kindle)

Unless otherwise indicated, Bible quotations are taken from the New International Version marked NIV: Copyright © 1984 by Zondervan Corporation.

Design and Layout by Mr. Michael J. Matulka of Basik Studios
Omaha, Nebraska USA

Published by Basik Studios (*www.gobasik.com*)
Omaha, Nebraska USA

Printed in the USA

Contents

Dedication

This book is dedicated to the following special people in my life:

My wife Cyprianna and my three daughters:
Tamara, Tonya and Amari, and all my Family:
Thanks for your unwavering belief in me.

Bahamas Faith Ministries International Intercessors:
Pastor Angie Achara, Pastor Gloria Seymour,
Dr. Ingrid Johnson, and the late Minister Alma Trottman.
&
The BFMI Diplomat Band and Worship Teams.

The Sanhedrin Council (my inner circle of friends):
Andrew & Kay Gardiner, Lionel & Lavon Harris,
Vince & Doretha Miller, Carl & Laverne Albury,
Hubert & Sharon Adderley, and Ade & Christine Doceomo;
Your continued expressions of love in words and actions
set the standard in our friendships.
You were uncles and aunts to our children, and
each one enjoyed a special relationship with you.

Worship God *Again*

Acknowledgments

I humbly acknowledge and thank the following persons for allowing me to serve my gift to them and the world:

Dr. Myles Munroe and Pastor Ruth Munroe, senior pastors. Thank you Pastor Myles for being my worship mentor, and thanks for allowing me to take our worship training conference to other nations.

Dr. Richard Pinder and Pastor Sheena Pinder, fellowship pastors. Thank you Pastor Rich for being a friend.
Pastors Henry and Sheila Frances, Pastors Jay and Euterpie Mullings, Dr. Dave Burrows and Pastor Angie Burrows, the Board of Governors, fellowship pastors, and ministers.

Special thanks to my close friends:

Bishop Neil C. Ellis, Pastor Mario Moxey, Charles and Ruth Brown, Lionel Harris, Dandria Scott, Dr. Ann Peterson Higgins, and my spiritual son, James Hepburn.

Dr. Pepe Ramnath, Dr. Ron Kenoly, Reverend Maurice Davis, and Beverly Dwyer.

Thanks to the following persons for their many years of ministerial support:

Minister Philip Gray and Minister Alvin Moss & Nadine Moss.
Rev. Nicole Ballosingh Holder of Trinidad and Tobago and Minister Judy Turnbull and Team of St. Thomas US Virgin Islands.

I am grateful for the help of two special friends/colleagues:

Marian Sturrup: Thanks for transcribing my last interview that was conducted by Dr. Lucile Richardson.

Dr. Lucile Richardson: Thank you for patiently working with me from the inception of this manuscript some 2-3 years prior to my last interview. I was encouraged by your visit to my home to work alongside me in recording my final thoughts and revelation about this new title.

Foreword

True Worship and Praise is a lifestyle. In *"WORSHIP GOD AGAIN"*, Dr. Mark Bethel reminds us over and over in many ways that we must actually live a life of quality worship in order to be the kind of worshippers that the Father is looking for.

In John chapter 4, our Savior reveals that worship is not just a good idea but a requirement of our Heavenly Father. In verse 24, our Messiah tells us how we must worship when He tells the woman at the Well that "The Father seeketh those who worship in Spirit and truth." The word 'seeketh' does not mean that He is trying to find someone who is worshipping that way. In the Greek Lexicon, "seeketh (zeteo)" means our Heavenly Father is requiring, demanding, expecting, and will not settle for anything less than a heart of love, honor, sincerity and respect from those who call themselves His children.

This book is not just for those in worship ministry, it is a must read for persons in any leadership role in ministry. When we take a close look at all of the major characters in the Scriptures, we see that they were worshippers. There is no substitute for a believer living a lifestyle of worship, continual praise, and thanks to our Creator.

In *"WORSHIP GOD AGAIN"*, Dr. Mark Bethel teaches us how to prepare for worship with a Kingdom understanding. He gives us insight regarding the Holy Spirit's role in our worship experience. He gives us clarity about what the Father expects from us, and the importance of authentic praise and worship. Mark shares new revelations about praise and worship that were given to him in the midst of his great trials and tests. He not only gives us concepts about worship and praise, he also gives us step by step instructions and personal testimonies of how true worship and praise carried him through the darkest days of his life.

His victories are an inspiration to those who know and love him. He is even candid about his mistakes and errors.

If you are a worshipper or one who desires to be a worshipper, this book will take you to a higher level in your praise and worship experience. It will help you to develop a closer relationship with our Creator. It will cause you to reexamine your present spiritual place and condition.

Our Father requires truth in our inward parts. However, that does not just happen. It requires a purging of all that is unpleasing to the Holy Spirit and an attitude of perpetual praise and worship along with continual prayer.

Dr. Mark Bethel's love for our Heavenly Father was unquestionable. His love for his family was undeniable. His talents were admired by everyone who witnessed his gifts. His leadership was intelligent, bold, and courageous. His heart was humble and submitted to his leaders and Scriptural principles. He was a man whom other men called "The Man". Dr. Mark Bethel was a General in the army of the Kingdom of Heaven.

Dr. Ron Kenoly
Ron Kenoly Ministries Inc.

Introduction

WORSHIP GOD AGAIN was formed in my heart since 2009. I spent a lot of time agonizing over the exact title until after my 2010 extensive illness, which gave me a different perspective about my own worship. This encounter has compelled me to begin searching God's Word for the true meaning of worship.

This book provides a kingdom understanding about worship and the Holy Spirit's role in our corporate and personal worship. I share how we need a more comprehensive understanding of authentic worship so we can teach others and lead them in the right direction.

If you have never understood the meaning of authentic worship and what is required to engage God's presence, this book will challenge you to examine your core convictions and philosophies that may be a hindrance to your relationship with God. You will have an opportunity to examine your core convictions about worship which are your fundamental beliefs.

Some worship leaders, musicians, and other Christians believe skill outranks spirituality. You will understand that there are several misguided convictions about skill and worship. Our goal should be to find out what God expects from us so our worship can become God-centered instead of people-centered.

I have seen people participating in worship that was not about God. They were the life of the party as if their worship was in honor of them. These observations led me to search God's Word for the true meaning of worship so you can experience His presence without any hindrances.

WORSHIP GOD AGAIN concludes with my personal testimony about an illness that became a mind-changing worship experience; one that I never knew existed. It is a special place in true worship that I find difficult to describe.

I share how I am in a new season of worship preparation and total surrender to God. There is no longer a concern for where, what, or how I did things in the past. The old things have passed away and HE has made all things new to me. I am worshipping God all over again in a new season, in a new place and a new time. There is no comparison! My best description would be that it is like worshipping God for the first time ever.

Chapter 1

WORSHIP WITH A
KINGDOM
UNDERSTANDING

For God is the King of all the earth;
sing praises in a skillful psalm and with understanding
- Psalm 47:7 (Amplified Bible)

You are walking along the beach across piles of rocks that look like they were placed there by someone who took the time to arrange them in piles. Among many random rock arrangements, the observation of stacked rocks leads you to the conclusion that some intelligent person arranged them. How much more is the complex arrangement of Creation? If it was formed by design, there must have been a designer.

The first book of the Bible guides us through the glorious process of Creation and the Creator. The Old Testament Book of Job tells how Job demanded answers to his excruciating trial, and God instructed him to go back and observe Creation. The prophet Isaiah asks the question of to whom then is equal to or like the Creator.

Isaiah 40:25-26
To whom will you compare me? Or who is my equal?" says the Holy
One. ²⁶ Lift up your eyes and look to the heavens: Who created
all these? He who brings out the starry host one by one and calls
forth each of them by name. Because of his great power and mighty
strength, not one of them is missing.

Psalm 47:7 says God is the King of all the earth, and we must sing praises to him with the understanding that He's not only our King, but He is the King over all the kings of the earth. If we are to sing praises to our God, we must understand the concept of a king and a kingdom. The word *god* is not a name, but a description. GOD means creator of everything. One of the names used to identify God is *Eloheim*, whom Dr. Myles Munroe defined as:

- *Self-Existing One* - is in itself and is conceived by itself, a natural whole; a complete individual being, in opposition to parts, properties, or modifications of such a being.

- *Self-Sustaining One* - is able to sustain one's self or itself independently.

- *Self-Sufficient One* - is free from external control and constraint. To be a god, one must be self-existing, self-sufficient, self- sustaining; one who needs nothing to exist (Munroe).

1 Timothy 1:17
Now to the King eternal, immortal, invisible, the only God, be honor and glory for ever and ever. Amen.

Praise is ascribed to God, as *the King eternal, immortal, invisible*. The word *eternal* means never-ending, timeless; immortal never dies, and *invisible* is concealed. This gives us a reason to pronounce Him great and show our admiration of his glorious attributes such as:

- Eternal, without beginning of days, end of life, or change of time.

- The Ancient of days (Dan. 7:9).

- Immortal and the original of immortality.
  He only has immortality (1st Tim. 6:16), for He cannot die.

- Invisible, for He cannot be seen with mortal eyes.

- The only wise God (Jude 1:25). His wisdom is infinite.

"To him be glory for ever and ever" is our way of saying we can never stop praising Him and giving honor to the One it is due (Rev. 5:12).

A KING

God created everything. He is the owner and ruler of the domain of heaven. The rightful owner or ruler of a domain is called a king, and the territory or domain over which the king rules is called a kingdom.

- A king is identified as one who possesses absolute, supreme and sovereign authority, and his control over a territory known as a kingdom.

- Everything in that territory belongs to Him and it functions under a monarchial system of governance.

- He is personally responsible and obligated to care for his subjects.

- His intent is to extend the kingdom of heaven on earth through mankind; to share his ruler-ship with mankind as ruler over the domain of earth. This made Jesus' mission on earth specifically to restore His kingdom as our inheritance.

Matt. 25:34
Then the King will say to those on his right, 'Come, you who are blessed by my Father; take your inheritance, the kingdom prepared for you since the creation of the world.'

I grew up in Nassau, Bahamas, under the rule of the British Empire, which gave me the opportunity to experience abiding by the rules of a monarchal system. Being immersed in the British culture and coming into the knowledge of Jesus Christ allowed me to compare the differences between the kingdom of Great Britain and the kingdom of God. Unlike Queen Elizabeth, who inherited her position from a long line of previous heads, Jehovah Eloheim is Creator, Ruler, and Owner of all creation. He was and is and is to come (Revelation 4:8).

LOVE FOR OUR KING

Love for our King compels us to worship Him with a love that also compels us to surrender our heart to Him. The word '*heart*' in the Western Hemisphere refers to our emotional feelings. For example, when a man says he loves a woman *with all his heart*, he is describing intense emotions.

The ancient Hebrew meaning of *heart* also refers to our emotions, but it includes our spiritual, mental, and physical life. The Hebrews viewed man as a total unit, and the word *heart* was understood in that context.

The Hebrew word for *heart* is *labab*, meaning "the midst, innermost, or hidden parts of anything." Some biblical phrases are:

- The *heart of the sea* (Exodus 15:8).

- The *heart of heaven* (Deuteronomy 4:11).

- The *heart of a tree* (2 Samuel 18:14).

- The *heart of the earth* (Matthew 12:40).

The Hebrew word *heart* also refers to *the seat of man's collective energies and the focus of his personal life*. The heart becomes the throne upon which life itself sits. When we worship God with all our heart, our worship should come from within the core of our being.

In The English Bible, one of the most common Greek words translated as heart is the word *kardia*. It refers to the center seat of both spiritual and physical life, and it carries the connotation of both soul and mind. Kardia was often used to refer to the mind as the foundation seat of human thoughts, passions, desires, appetites, affections, purposes, and endeavors. This is required of every citizen of the kingdom of God, but more so the worship leader (The English Bible).

The Greek scholar Robinson believes that kardia refers to the personality, inner life, and character of an individual (Rines, (1920).) From this study, I have concluded with a general definition for the word *heart* being "the core of a person's body, mind, emotions, personality, character, and spirit." So when the Lord tells us to give Him our heart, He is asking for our entire life.

The heart is the most important body organ. Without it, other organs, processes, and functions would cease, and so would life. It is located approximately in the center of our chest. Likewise our spiritual heart is located in the center of our thoughts, words, actions, and ministry, motivating everything in life. It is designed for us to love God and show love to the world. This love can express itself in many ways such as changed lives, wherein people become obedient to the will of God.

OUR LOVE FOR GOD IS SEEN THROUGH VISIBLE WORSHIP OF HIM.

One of the ways that love for God is seen in the Bible is through the unmistakable visible worship of Him. When believers gather together for God's purposes, a major way that the presence of God becomes evident and clear among us is when we reach out to Him on one accord in worship. We are saying the same thing together while calling out to His glorious name.

We worship God as our King with an understanding of the concept of a king and a kingdom. We give our King the worship He deserves, the attention He desires, and the allegiance He demands.

- **Give your King the WORSHIP He deserves.**

1 Peter 2:17
Show proper respect to everyone, love the family of believers, fear God, honor the emperor.

1 Chronicles 16:29
Ascribe to the Lord the glory due his name; bring an offering and come before him. Worship the Lord in the splendor of his[a] holiness.

- **Give your King the Attention He desires.**

1 Samuel 3:10 (NASB)
Then the LORD came and stood and called as at other times, 'Samuel! Samuel!' And Samuel said, 'Speak, for Your servant is listening.'

A family was riding down the road one afternoon when the husband and child were trying to talk to his wife at the same time. Finally the wife said, "I can't listen to two people at the same time!" The child replied, "I don't see why not. You have two ears!" Often we try to "listen" to God and the world at the same time. Even though we do have two ears, such a dual allegiance is not possible. (Parent Life, July 1998, p. 44)

- **Give your King the Allegiance He demands.**

Philippians 3:20
But our citizenship is in heaven. And we eagerly await a Savior from there, the Lord Jesus Christ,

Saying "Jesus is Lord" means we give absolute loyalty, allegiance, and obedience to Him. Allegiance to Christ means we are called to honor God in every aspect of our lives.

<u>Luke 14:33 (NASB)</u>

So therefore, any one of you who does not renounce all that he has cannot be my disciple.

The Lord does not want the first place in your life, He wants all of your life." Billy Graham said "Christ will not take 70% or 90% or even 99%. He wants our all." (Graham)

<u>Matthew 6:24</u>

"No one can serve two masters; for either he will hate the one and love the other, or else he will be loyal to the one and despise the other. You cannot serve God and mammon."

FAITH IS REQUIRED OF US IF WE ARE TO PLEASE OUR KING.

The operative ingredient to succeed in God's kingdom is called faith. The Bible tells us that faith is required of us if we are to please God. So if we do not have faith in the King, then it is impossible to please Him.

<u>Hebrews 11:6</u>

And without faith it is impossible to please God, because anyone who comes to him must believe that he exists and that he rewards those who earnestly seek him.

Developing faith comes through studying the Bible, which contains our guidelines on how to live and understand the King's mindset so we can be approved by Him (II Tim. 2:15).

Over the years, there has been a rediscovery that the kingdom of God is not something mythical but an actual spiritual country with a system of governance, a culture, constitution, an army, and a common wealth, made available to its citizens. In light of our rediscovery of God as our Creator and King allows us to approach Him in our worship with a kingdom understanding.

Chapter 2

THE HOLY SPIRIT'S ROLE

"In an effort to get the work of the Lord done
we often lose contact with the Lord of the work."
- A. W. Tozer

The Holy Spirit fulfills a vital role in our worship that reveals God's work through Christ. Worship without the Holy Spirit is not possible. The worship sanctuary reveals the Spirit's presence when boundaries are formed and members are unified. There is a conviction of sin that ensures the integrity of the worshipers and strengthens them to serve one another. Such unification puts no confidence in the flesh, removes the spirit of idolatry, and promotes true worship of God.

Worship is a central emphasis of the Bible from Genesis to Revelation. Adam and Eve were commissioned to serve in the Garden, God's first sanctuary on the earth. The patriarchs marked their journeys by their devotion at God's altar. For forty years Israel used the Tabernacle as its compass when marching; it became the center for their temporary camp. Once Israel had a king, Solomon's Temple became the perpetual reminder that God, not the king, had the preeminent place in the nation. It was God who created and redeemed us so that He might receive worship from His Creation. He made worship the goal of His work.

CORPORATE & PERSONAL WORSHIP

The Holy Spirit's role in corporate worship becomes a function of our response rather than an objective theological reality. Sometimes we miss the more basic and important roles that the Holy Spirit assumes whenever God's people gather to enter worship.

The Old Testament provides many examples of God's condemnation and rejection of worship that forgot or ignored His expectations. Any discussion of corporate worship must start with a prerequisite demonstrated in the Old and New Testament. God only accepts worship offered within a covenant framework.

The word *covenant* simply describes an explicit relationship between two parties, in this case, God and human beings. The relationship has clearly defined prerequisites and commitments. Sometimes both parties to the covenant must keep all the commitments for the covenant to remain in force - a "conditional" covenant, while at other times God promises to uphold the covenant with no mention being made of the other party's responsibilities-an "unconditional" or unilateral covenant.

Conditions do not change in the New Testament. Jesus criticized his contemporaries for their failure to fulfill God's requirements before worshipping (Matthew 5:21-24; 6:1-24). We speak of personal worship such as practiced in personal devotions and corporate worship experienced in a worship service.

Biblically and historically, personal acts of worship were merely on one end of the spectrum; corporate acts of worship were at the other end. So-called personal worship was but a stepping stone to worship offered within the gathered community of God's people. Personal worship was insufficient in itself to honor God as He desired.

WORSHIP IN SPIRIT AND TRUTH

Jesus' encounter with the Samaritan woman defined New Testament worship as offered "in spirit and truth" (John 4:24).

- **In truth** describes the objective prerequisite of conformity to the revelation of God for humanity in worship (His holiness as the one true God and how He has revealed He is to be worshiped).

- **In spirit** denotes the subjective prerequisite: the integrity and sincerity required of every worshiper. Jesus' use of spirit may include the work of the Holy Spirit. Hebrews 10:5-7 emphasizes the same.

Both Old and New Testaments agree that God only accepts worship offered by a humble and committed servant under His covenant who is qualified by the Holy Spirit's presence in our lives and in our worship.

THE WORSHIPPING COMMUNITY

The Holy Spirit's second function in worship is His creation of the worshipping community. Biblical covenants always involve a group. God redeems individuals, but His redemptive goal is the creation of a people, a community.

In the Old Testament God acted as He promised, redeemed his people, and then brought them together into a community of persons in the covenant (Ps. 106:4; Isa. 11:12). An Israelite judged by God took the form of isolation from the community. Individuals were sent out to be alone; groups were dispersed. Those judged were then unable to gather for the worship God had stipulated.

Psalm 106:4
Remember me, Lord, when you show favor to your people, come to
my aid when you save them,

Isaiah 11:12
He will raise a banner for the nations and gather the exiles of Israel;
he will assemble the scattered people of Judah from the four quarters
of the earth.

For believers, this experience of community becomes a reality through the
Holy Spirit indwelling each covenant member.

- He unites believers into a single people, the community of
  Christ. At one level, the Spirit connects the members of a local
  congregation together into a functioning whole. At a higher
  level, He connects all believers both as individuals and local
  communities to all others everywhere.

- He erases the separation of space and geography between each
  congregation. And, at the highest level, the same Spirit bonds
  those who have been divided from the earthly community by
  death with their brothers and sisters yet living on the earth.

- He brings the Church scattered throughout time and space into
  an organic whole. His presence in our worship affirms that we
  are not alone. We are surrounded by a great cloud of witnesses in
  heaven (Hebrews 12:1).

IN UNITY

The first statements of unity among humanity represent a rebellion against
God's order and rule. So God destroyed all life with a catastrophic flood

(Genesis chapters 6-9). Later at Babel, God foresaw that the impulses and achievements of a sinful, unified humanity would only produce a similar rebellion against His rule (Gen. 8:21) requiring the same judgment. He frustrated humanity's rebellious plan by implementing a language division (Gen. 11:1-9). These subgroups scattered over the earth as God had planned. Over time, geographical, racial, and cultural distinctions prevented humanity from achieving such unity again.

The unity of believers under the rule and direction of the Holy Spirit functions as a prerequisite for the corporate worship that God accepts. It shows our submission to the Holy Spirit's work and our integrity under the new covenant. Without functional unity nurtured by the Holy Spirit, there can be no acceptable corporate worship.

INTEGRITY

The Holy Spirit preserves our integrity as community members in worship. He provokes and judges those things which violate the demands of the covenant, pollute the holiness of the sanctuary, disturb its communal identity, mar its functional unity, or disqualify its witness and offerings. His presence examines, reveals, and convicts us of our personal transgressions of God's standards. He prompts us to maintain our covenantal integrity before God, for without this our worship offering is disqualified. The Spirit preserves our identity as the pure, unified people whose worship will be accepted by God.

Our worship is empowered by the following:

- His presence defines the members of the community.

- He forms the community itself as a sanctuary for the worship of the living God.

- He empowers each individual to contribute to the unity that alone testifies to the deity of the Savior.

- He provokes the purity of the community (as a people and as a sanctuary).

The Holy Spirit also gives integrity to worship offered by the corporate gathering of God's people. Without the essential works of the Holy Spirit, worship offered by people is not accepted by Him.

DIRECTED TO THE FATHER

Our worship expressions are directed to the Father, expressing appreciation for His works of creation and redemption. Worship is offered in the person of the Son, "in Jesus' name," an expression that speaks to the virtue of his ascended person, and the authority He has conferred on those who are his. The Spirit's presence legitimizes our worship; the Holy Spirit bonds us to our Savior and guarantees our salvation.

BRIDGE BETWEEN WORSHIP AND ETHICS

The Holy Spirit creates the bridge between worship and ethics. They do not compete and they are not isolated components. The Holy Spirit strengthens us to fulfill our covenantal obligations as affirmed in our worship. This connection is described in Isaiah chapter 6 with his vision of God and of the celestial worship that surrounded him.

Isaiah 6:1-4
In the year that King Uzziah died, I saw the Lord, high and exalted, seated on a throne; and the train of his robe filled the temple. 2 Above him were seraphim, each with six wings: With two wings they

covered their faces, with two they covered their feet, and with two they were flying. 3 And they were calling to one another: "Holy, holy, holy is the Lord Almighty; the whole earth is full of his glory." 4 At the sound of their voices the doorposts and thresholds shook and the temple was filled with smoke.

Verse 5 shows it produced in the prophet a deep sense of inadequacy and sin:

"Woe to me!" I cried. "I am ruined! For I am a man of unclean lips, and I live among a people of unclean lips, and my eyes have seen the King, the Lord Almighty."

But it was remedied supernaturally in verses 6-7:

Then one of the seraphim flew to me with a live coal in his hand, which he had taken with tongs from the altar. 7 With it he touched my mouth and said, "See, this has touched your lips; your guilt is taken away and your sin atoned for."

Our response to the Holy Spirit in our worship should be that of Richard Baxter, who, in The Reformed Liturgy, encourages us to pray that the Holy Spirit would draw us to Christ, unite us in love, strengthen us in praise, confirm us in obedience, and seal us unto eternal life (Baxter, 1961).

OUR TRUE WORSHIP LEADER

The Holy Spirit enables us to worship so we can become like Jesus. Worship is not a piece of a puzzle being worked into our lives. The Holy Spirit is like the tiny lines you see throughout a puzzle that have been put together. Our worship joins those pieces into forming a whole.

Worship is not an event. It becomes our lifestyle. Our worship joins the pieces of our lives together as a whole. It is a part of everything we do.

> John 16:14
> *He will glorify me because it is from me that he will receive what he will make known to you.*

Worship should be our response when the Spirit gives us a revelation of Christ's glory. He will lead us in worship enabling us to worship like Jesus. The Holy Spirit is our Worship Leader. He will bring glory to God. He will exalt and magnify Jesus; He will make the glory of Christ known to you and me.

Chapter 3

AUTHENTIC WORSHIP

If you seek authenticity for authenticity's sake
you are no longer authentic.
-Jean Paul Sartre

Around the world there is a surging revival of worship. Growing churches are typically known, at least in part, for their dynamic worship services. Some focus on entertaining and amusing the congregation or being more concerned about not offending people rather than desiring to please God. There needs to be a more comprehensive understanding of authentic worship so we can teach others and lead them in the right direction.

Authentic worship requires communicating God's mind and intent and having a genuine relationship with Him.

Having a genuine relationship with God is grounded in an awareness that our sins have been forgiven so we can have eternal life. It also requires our faith to be anchored in the glory and majesty of our Creator. The Apostle Paul describes an act of authentic worship as the placing of our bodies on the altar as a sacrifice to God.

Romans 12:1
Therefore, I urge you, brothers, in view of God's mercy, to offer your bodies as living sacrifices, holy and pleasing to God this is your spiritual act of worship.

Our *bodies* represent the totality of our life. It is the offering of all that we are, and all that we do, as an act of worship unto God. Our prayer then becomes "Oh, Lord, I offer my body (total life) to you as an act of authentic worship." This is our spiritual act of worship.

Paul gathers up the totality of life and presents it to God as a great offering of spiritual worship. That includes our daily work, recreation, study, relationships, every thought and imagination. It includes every day of the week and not just Sunday worship. Every aspect of corporate celebration and praise is included. Good times, sickness, heartbreak, and financial despair - all are gathered and offered to the Lord as an acceptable sacrifice, which is pleasing in His sight. This is authentic worship. It is the totality of life that Paul presents to God as a great offering of spiritual worship.

Romans 12:2
Do not conform any longer to the pattern of this world, but be transformed by the renewing of your mind."

Authentic worship reflects transformation;
a makeover, becoming the opposite of what used to be.

Being authentic in our work means we refuse to enter into a conforming pattern; our minds have been renewed. We no longer pattern after the world's way of doing things. Paul's meaning says we cannot allow ourselves to be poured into a mold that fits the world's design. If so, we will bear its imprint in ways such as customs, habits, values, religious beliefs and ideologies. Instead, we are called to be transformed into a life of purity and holiness. This lifestyle comes when worship flows out of a renewed mind.

The psalmist asked a question about who may stand in God's holy presence and He gave the answer.

Psalm 24:3-4

Who may ascend the hill of the LORD? Who may stand in his holy place? He who has clean hands and a pure heart, who does not lift up his soul to an idol or swear by what is false.

Authentic worship exposes every covered sin and drives the worshipper to an altar of repentance.

God's will is achieved when we offer to Him a holy life; a life that is cleansed, undefiled, separate from the world and aligned with the word of God. It insists on the continual renewing of the mind, which comes from spending time in the Word and applying it to our daily life. There is no quick fix; we are constantly renewing our minds as we deal with life's challenges. Temptations will come, but with God's help and by His grace, we are able to overcome them and live a life of holiness.

Romans 12:2b

Then you will be able to test and approve what God's will is his good, pleasing and perfect will.

Authentic worship is the gathering of all of our life, not some but all, and presenting it to the Lord as a spiritual act of worship.

Authentic worship is the totality of our being. Nothing is left uncovered. It is when we want God's perfect will to be achieved rather than ours. His will is always perfect.

Take time to examine the authenticity of your spiritual life. You should be able to look at the people around you to see whether they are drawn to faith by your life. Those who cross your path should recognize that there is a difference in the way you live. Your co-workers, family members, neighbors and friends, should see the "fruit of the Spirit" growing in your life. They should be able to see that you are real. There should not be any impurity mixed with your faith.

In Paul's letter to the Galatians, he describes what a life looks like when the Holy Spirit is active. The evidence will be seen by the fruit we bear. The key is being authentic, real, and not trying to appear perfect.

> Galatians 5:22-23
> *But the fruit of the Spirit is love, joy, peace, forbearance, kindness, goodness, faithfulness, [23] gentleness and self-control. Against such things there is no law.*

Nobody likes a phony, and if you think you are fooling everybody, then the only person you are probably fooling is yourself. I assure you that you are not fooling God. If you want people to think you never struggle, then you are not authentic. You are just wearing a mask.

In ancient Greece, great theatrical events and plays were held in large amphitheaters. Actors did not have microphones to make their voices heard, and they did not have cameras to magnify their images, so they invented a system by developing large masks, which made them look like the characters they portrayed. Built into the masks were megaphones to amplify their voices. The actors on stage were behind their masks, and they became somebody else called the *hypocrite.*

Some people's lives are nothing more than a big act. They are being hypocritical, fake, and false. God wants to change us but not superficially. He calls us to be conformed to the image of His Son. It is more than just changing the way we look. He wants to clean us up from the very core of our being.

When we come into the sanctuary to worship, we need to concentrate on God. We cannot worship Him if our focus is on someone or something else. Doing that makes us nothing more than a hypocrite! Therefore, our heart must be focused on Jesus in worship.

Mark 7:6
He replied, "Isaiah was right when he prophesied about you hypocrites; as it is written: "'These people honor me with their lips, but their hearts are far from me.

SIGNS OF AUTHENTIC WORSHIP

When the church decides as individuals to become authentic worshippers, we will see a revival in our community.

Here are some signs of authentic worship:

a) It hinders the enemy from invading the church and the Gospel.

b) It uplifts believers and promotes an excitement for the Lord.

c) It drives out sin and bondage from the lives of many.

d) It causes the believer to experience the Lord in intimate heart to heart ways.

e) It brings fresh revelations of Jesus.

f) It brings us into the presence of the Lord.

g) It prepares our hearts for revival.

- Reading from Isaiah 32:3-5, this is what will happen when revival is unlocked and flows into the church.

    o *Then the eyes of those who see will no longer be closed, and the ears of those who hear will listen.*

o *The mind of the rash will know and understand and
the stammering tongue will be fluent and clear.*

o *No longer will the fool be called noble nor the
scoundrel be highly respected.*

INFLUENCING THE WORLD
TOWARD GODLINESS

Jesus calls us to influence the world toward godliness. To do it we must be authentic in our relationship with Him. We must have faith in Him that changes us from the inside out. This is how we influence others for Christ. They need to see the difference in us. We must be the good news before we share the Good News.

I heard a story about a preacher who was building a wooden trellis to support a climbing vine. As he was pounding away, he noticed that a little boy was watching him. The youngster did not say a word, so the preacher kept on working thinking the boy would leave but he remained quietly observing. The preacher was quite pleased at the thought that the boy was admiring his work. Finally he asked the boy, "Are you trying to pick up some pointers on gardening?" "No," the boy replied. "I'm just waiting to hear what a preacher says when he smashes his thumb with a hammer."

This story shows how our lives always have an impact upon others either positively or negatively. What we say and do influences others like salt influences foods. God wants our lives to have the positive influence.

BECOME THE SALT INFLUENCE

Matthew 5:13

You are the salt of the earth. But if the salt loses its saltiness, how can it be made salty again? It is no longer good for anything, except to be thrown out and trampled underfoot.

Our lives should be like salt; a seasoning, a preservative. Unless salt is brought in contact with another object its influence is wasted. It must become invisible to have a visible effect. When salt is rubbed onto and into meat, or added to food, it becomes invisible then it becomes what it was intended do- influence the flavor.

Salt alone is nothing more than little fine particles. If it just sits in the salt shaker, it is of no use much like Believers who become complacent and refuse to take a moral stand or share their faith. They are sitting in a shaker, and the Holy Spirit has to shake them up and make them uncomfortable as He works out the compromises in their life. He wants them to experience authentic worship by living authentic lives.

I hope your salt is not sitting on the shelf knowing you were born to fulfill a divine assignment in life. You must become an authentic flavor, leaving no room to play the role of a hypocrite. You are called to live a life of holiness so your worship can be authentic.

Worship God *Again*

Chapter 4

CORE CONVICTIONS ABOUT
SKILL & WORSHIP

The way of fools seems right to them,
but the wise listen to advice.
- Proverbs 12:15

Worship is the one part of church life that you would expect worship leaders and musicians to understand. Yet, when I do worship training seminars and ask the leaders to tell me what convictions shape their worship, there is an awkward silence. It seems as though I have asked a question that is too difficult to answer.

So what are core convictions? The word '*core*' simply means essential, central, fundamental, and basic, primary or underlying. It suggests those things that are the very heart of what worship is, or at least what you believe worship is. The word '*conviction*' means beliefs, principles, opinions, persuasions or views. So your core convictions will be your fundamental beliefs about worship.

If you do not know what your convictions are about worship, you will not have any anchors to hold steadfast and sure when conflict breaks out over worship. I suggest that you find some time to write down your personal core convictions about worship. Church leaders should be included in this assignment. Children and youth should also be included since they are part of the worshipping community.

My numerous international travels have afforded me the opportunity to observe worship in a variety of venues. I recall one event where the singers and musicians were admirable but not spiritually connected. In the end, I met with the worship leader to discuss a few challenges that he encountered during the event. He said most of his musicians were from all walks of life. They also played with other local bands in night clubs and bars. There was never a complaint from them about the monitors or other equipment on stage, because they were excited about playing in a nice Christian atmosphere.

SKILL VERSUS SPIRITUALITY

My friend's singers and musicians were highly skilled, since the worship leader's philosophy was that "skill outranks spirituality." Worship leaders, musicians, and other believers who believe skill outranks spirituality have misguided philosophies and convictions that lead to an imitation of worship.

Five Major Misguided Convictions About Skill:

1. It is okay to practice ungodly behavior.

2. A musical gift should not be controlled by those who do not have the same gift they possess.

3. Skill is above the law of integrity, loyalty, honesty, transparency, and dedication to God.

4. It is okay to dress seductively; appearance does not matter.

5. Skillful musicians can be disrespectful to spiritual leadership without having to repent or be corrected.

My friend's singers and musicians may not have known or understood God's first Commandment given to the Israelites that they shall have no other gods before Him (Exod. 20:3). But there is nothing too hard for God. The Holy Spirit can cultivate their unreserved hearts. He has the power to touch lives and draw a single-minded devotion that some will reject while others will embrace it. When the transformation is complete, believers will no longer ask, "What is the minimum required of me? "How much can I get by with?" Instead, they will ask: "What is the most I can give?" Some will say, "I want to give all."

When you discover the pleasure of living for one thing, you will not desire anything less. God wants you to worship Him alone. That means entering His presence bowed down in a position of humility while declaring He is king over your life. You must examine your own self to see who and what you have put ahead of God. He must be first and foremost in your life. Believe that He exists and that He will reward you for earnestly seeing Him. God will meet with you when you come bowed humbly before Him. Being in His presence is all you need. No matter how much pain and suffering, it is God's presence that brings healing.

Heb. 11:6
And without faith it is impossible to please God, because anyone who comes to him must believe that he exists and that he rewards those who earnestly seek him.

Four Major Misguided Convictions About Worship

Here are four misguided convictions about worship that are dispelled through the word of God and living testimonies:

1. Worship is just singing songs.

2. Worship is a sacrifice, not sacrificial.

3. Worship focuses more on the people than on God.

4. Worship is for our entertainment.

WORSHIP IS NOT JUST SINGING SONGS.

Songs are just a means to help create an environment for the worship experience. We must be careful in knowing the words that we sing, because they are confessions that may be in right alignment with God's Word. People get healed, delivered, and set free by His Spirit while worshipping God.

Worship songs should only be about God. We place Him above all else because He is worth it! We respond to Him with all of our life, with everything that we have been given, and all that He is. So, if we enter a worship service and raise our hands and lift our voices, but we do not stretch these same hands out to feed the hungry and clothe the naked, fight for the poor and the oppressed, then you and I have worshipped a singer or a song, but we have NOT worshipped God.

WORSHIP IS NOT A SACRIFICE; IT IS SACRIFICIAL.

Psalms 51:16-17
You do not delight in sacrifice, or I would bring it; you do not take pleasure in burnt offerings. The sacrifices of God are a broken spirit; a broken and contrite heart, O God, you will not despise.

God owns the cattle on a thousand hills. He does not need our cattle. He does not need our gifts at all. He is much more interested in our heart. In John 4:20, Jesus is talking to the Samaritan woman and there is a conversation on worship. He says in verse 23 that the Father is seeking those who will worship Him in spirit and in truth. He is looking for people who will lay everything down before Him.

God's Word admonishes us to present our bodies as a living sacrifice, holy and pleasing to Him, which is our reasonable service. It is how we are to properly worship our heavenly Father (Romans 12:1).

We worship God by laying down our lives, our will and our feelings in reverence, respect, and honor to Him. That means we are saying our life is not our own; we belong to God. This should be the attitude of our heart, and our outward actions should be a reflection of the things within our heart.

WORSHIP DOES NOT FOCUS ON PEOPLE, BUT ON GOD ALONE.

Close your eyes for a minute and remove your thoughts from the people around you or your physical environment. Now talk to God:

> *"Here I am Lord God. I make a decision right now to present my life to you. I exalt You and I praise You. Instead of looking at myself, I choose to direct my mind towards You Lord, the Almighty and Exalted One. I surrender to You Lord."*

Talk to God instead of sharing everything with your neighbor or a friend. You can meet with Him as you are. Just remember who He is. Do not desire to speak with someone else about God because of their ministerial position. It cannot be because they work for God; you need to speak directly with Him. He is in your midst saying, "Here I am waiting to hear you talk to Me." Redirect your focus to the thoughts of God rather than on the thoughts of others. Your prayers are not going to them.

Sometimes people pray nice prayers without having touched the heart of God. It is like a performance or a ritual. Every word is already written like a script, which is nice if you want to share your thoughts in writing, but you should not be limited only to your notes. Your time of worship is where you will experience His power flowing. Do not be discouraged; do not give up. Yield all of you to God and talk to Him by saying, "I'm for You Lord, You have all of me." Speak to God from your heart. Take the first step by coming to your heavenly

Father, the Holy and Almighty God. Let Him know that you are bowing before Him as your Master and King, not in words but in total reality.

WORSHIP IS NOT FOR OUR ENTERTAINMENT.

There is an erroneous idea that the main purpose for attending worship is to get something out of the service, rather than going to church to give our worship to God. This is a selfish motive on our part. We cannot be satisfied with worship when our emphasis is not on the right object of worship. We want to do our own thing in worship that makes us happy and feel good.

The world is filled with events designed to appeal to our emotions and entertain us. Some people are entertainment-oriented. They have many forms of amusement that are brought into their worship. But they seem to forget that the purpose for worship is to bring glory and honor to God; it is not to entertain ourselves. We have choirs that sing to us and concerts that provide entertainment.

WORSHIP IS NEVER INTENDED TO BE A SPECTATOR'S EVENT.

Worship requires participants - not spectators. A spectator does not understand all that is involved in a game like the one who participates. Spectators believe they can make a difference in the game while remaining in their seats. They tend to criticize or critique the efforts of participants.

Participants boldly declare God's Word with confidence (Jer. 20:9). They are excited about helping fulfill God's assignment. Being a participant is not just for our benefit. Something great happens when we become participants instead of spectators. We dare not become spectators, because God is our only

Spectator. These two roles cannot be reversed; people will expect God's divine will to conform to what seems right in their own eyes.

WORSHIP IS HOLY AND SACRED.

We must never corrupt worship with entertainment and getting what we want out of the service. This selfish motive only pleases and gratifies ourselves. The sacredness of worship must not be sacrificed on altars of entertainment-oriented quartets, choirs, and other entertainment groups. God wants us to be participants, not observers; God-centered, not people-centered. We must open our mouth and offer a sacrifice of praise to Him from our lips (Hebrews 13:15).

Our worship must never be based on the belief that skill outranks spirituality, or the misguided philosophies and convictions that worship is just singing songs, sacrifice rather than sacrificial, focused more on people than on God, or for our entertainment. Being God-centered is the only way our worship can be meaningful and spiritually uplifting. That is what He requires of us.

Chapter 5

GOD'S EXPECTATIONS

True worship leaders worship the Lord at all times
and use songs only when necessary.
- Gangai Victor

The world desires to participate in a "more entertaining" worship, and when that is not what they experience, they say we are failing to worship God in spirit and in truth. Such thinking is not scriptural. Our goal should be to find out what God expects from us so our worship can become God-centered instead of people-centered.

Here are eight things that God requires us to demonstrate in our lives:

1. Giving Everything - not holding anything back, giving and surrendering all;

2. Becoming Preoccupied with Him;

3. Faithfulness;

4. Trust, Reliance, Confidence;

5. Love;

6. Obedience;

7. Purity - not selfish; and

8. Humility.

1) *Give Everything*

God expects us to give everything – not holding anything back; giving and surrendering all. *Surrender* may not be a popular word in your vocabulary, because it implies loss and defeat to those who give everything. However, we are called to surrender, which is the essence of our daily worship.

Biblical history tells us that giving up everything without holding back involves a lot of will and desire. Genesis chapter 22 is the story of Abraham's calling to sacrifice his son, Isaac, who had to show willingness; he had to give up something. Abraham had to give it something with the promise of gaining something. Isaac had to give up something to be willing to lose something. In the New Testament, the apostle Paul gave himself to God and Christ came to live in him, so Paul gained more than he gave up (Gal. 2:17-19, 20-21).

2) *Become Preoccupied with Him*

Acts 18:5
When Silas and Timothy came from Macedonia, Paul devoted himself exclusively to preaching, testifying to the Jews that Jesus was the Messiah.

Becoming immersed with God means you fully understand what Jesus has done for you. It says you are sold out with your belief in Him. If we could learn anything from Jesus' disciples, it would be that you do not need to know everything to drop your nets and follow Him. They were sold out to His vision to go into every man's world and proclaim the Good News of the Gospel of the Kingdom.

3)   *Faithfulness*

Webster's Dictionary defines faithful as "maintaining allegiance; constant; loyal; marked by or showing a strong sense of duty or responsibility; conscientious; accurate; reliable; exact." (Webster's New World Dictionary). The Hebrew word for "faithfulness" is *emunah*, which literally means "firmness," figuratively means "security" and morally means "fidelity." (Strong's Concordance).

Faithfulness means we must love Christ supremely. We must be willing to give up all earthly possessions, forsake all earthly friends, and obey Him above all others including our own carnal desires.

God Himself is the model we must study as an example of faithfulness. His faithfulness seems to have been Paul's favorite subject. He writes of it in his first epistle (I Thessalonians) and again in what may have been his last (II Timothy). Paul proved it in a thousand dangers and struggles; he found that, when all was said and done, God never failed him.

When we are faithful to Christ, He does some wonderful things in us through His Spirit. Faithfulness is a fruit that seems to be sorely lacking in our society and in the church. When the fruit of faithfulness is growing in us, it will make our lives and the lives of those around us so much better. It will be something that other people will take notice of. Faithfulness is a fruit that other people desperately want to see in the lives of those around them.

4)   *Trust, Reliance, Confidence*

Psalm 125:1
Those who trust in the Lord are like Mount Zion, which cannot be shaken but endures forever.

Deuteronomy 31:6

Be strong and courageous. Do not be afraid or terrified because of them, for the LORD your God goes with you; he will never leave you nor forsake you.

When we as believers put our trust completely in God and let Him handle the affairs of our life, we will always succeed, because God never fails. He always delivers, and He always has our best interest at heart. The psalmist says we will not be moved or shaken.

The key is to totally trust God, and not have an ounce of doubt in us; we cannot waiver. He is faithful to those who are faithful to Him. We must have confidence in knowing God cannot lie and He always keeps His promise to us. Sometimes our human reasoning gets in the way of our understanding. That is why God tells us to trust Him with all our heart and not rely on our own understanding.

Proverbs 3:5-6

Trust in the Lord with all your heart and lean not on your own understanding; ⁶ in all your ways submit to him, and he will make your paths straight.

5) *Love*

Someone once said: A bell is not a bell until you ring it. A song is not a song until you sing it. And love in your heart is not love until you give it away. That is what God wants us to do with His love that is in our hearts. He wants it to be completely unconditional, self-less, and with complete acceptance of others without finding fault or being judgmental.

- *Love is completely unconditional.*

Love has no conditions. If our love is dependent upon the other person acting and speaking the things we want to hear, then that kind of love is conditional.

- *Love is self-less.*

Love does not want anything in return. We love for the sake of love. When we love people, we should not expect them to fill our needs, love us back, and all those types of other things. If that is what we are looking for, then we are just using them.

- *Love is complete acceptance.*

It is when we allow others to be themselves without any belief that they aren't good enough and without believing that they would be "better" if they were different.

God's goal in sending his Son from heaven to earth was not to condemn you or to show you how bad you are, or how unworthy or hopeless you are. His only desire in sending his Son was to show you His love and draw you into a love relationship with Himself.

A child was once trying to quote from John 3:16 in the King James Version, which says, "his only begotten Son." But the child misquoted it and said, "his only forgotten Son." It was a mistake in speech that carried more truth than we would care to admit. Our job as Kingdom citizens is to help the world remember Him and know Him by our unconditional, self-less love that shows complete acceptance of others.

6) Obedience

Obedience is an act of worship. Our obedience flows from a heart of gratitude for the grace we have received from the Lord. The general concept relates to hearing and obeying a higher authority. Holman says obedience means "to hear God's Word and act accordingly." (Holman's Illustrated Bible Dictionary).

Biblical obedience means to hear, trust, submit, and surrender to God and obey his Word. In the Ten Commandments, we see how important the concept of obedience is to God. Deuteronomy 11:26–28 says: "Obey and you will be blessed. Disobey and you will be cursed." In the New Testament, we learn through the example of Jesus Christ that believers are called to a life of obedience.

7) *Pure – Not Selfish*

> Philippians 4:8
> *Finally, brothers and sisters, whatever is true, whatever is noble, whatever is right, whatever is pure, whatever is lovely, whatever is admirable – if anything is excellent or praiseworthy – think about such things.*

> Matthew 5:8
> *Blessed are the pure in heart, for they will see God.*

Some people may ask "Why we don't see God's power in our churches anymore?" I believe it is because of the impure hearts. God cannot use a polluted vessel (James 3:11-12). This passage refers to the tongue, but the principle is the same.

A polluted spring cannot produce fresh water. God has called us to purity and holiness – not selfishness. We cannot experience His power without an unselfish life of purity. It doesn't matter what impurities we have, Jesus has the power to make us free in Him. The problem is that when He sets us free, if we return to bondage we are no better off. This key is to develop a personal relationship with Him. Without that relationship, everything else is limited because we are limited in our own strength.

8) *Humble*

Matthew 15:25 (KJV)
*Then came she and worshipped (knelt before) him, saying, Lord,
help me!*

The real essence of worship is the bowing of our self and lying prostrate before God. Worship requires getting rid of fleshly pride that wants to assert its own way. You are recognizing your total dependence and total abandonment to God. It is a position where you acknowledge and depend on Him.

Micah 6:8
*He has shown all you people what is good. And what does the LORD
require of you? To act justly and to love mercy and to walk humbly
with your God.*

Being humble keeps you from showing others how you worship God. Your worship should only be between you and Him, so He can be the One who puts the spotlight on you in your due season.

1 Peter 5:6
*Humble yourselves, therefore, under God's mighty hand, that he may
lift you up in due time.*

We must desire to live a God-centered life instead of being people-centered. Our lives should measure up to God's expectations by giving everything, surrendering all, and becoming totally preoccupied with Him. It requires us to be faithful and trusting God with full confidence. We must walk in love and obedience with an unselfish heart of humility. When we do these things, our worship will be pleasing to God.

Chapter 6

OUR GREATEST HINDRANCES

My people are destroyed from lack of knowledge.
- Hosea 4:6

Imagine being invited to an event in honor of someone and discovering the honored guest was not the person being celebrated. You knew you were in the right place at the right time, but the honoree was not the focus of the event. Instead, the entire celebration was all about the participants.

I have studied worship and served as a worship leader for many years, and I have seen people participating in worship that was not about God. He was not their focal point. Sadly it was all about them. They were the life of the party as if their worship was in honor of them. That was their epitome of worship. These observations led me to search God's word for the true meaning of worship, because if our worship is about us then we will never reach God to experience His presence.

There can be times when our worship will be hindered and God might not choose to accept our praise and worship. These usually are the times of ongoing sin in our lives; times when we are deliberately disobedient to Him day after day, which can affect His acceptance of our worship. My prayer is that we would worship God in Spirit and Truth. Come to worship ready to give to God and hear from Him.

Many areas of our lives provide opportunities to hide inward sin from others, but worship is one thing that you cannot give to God while hiding continual sin. You may "do" the motions of worship, but the heart doesn't lie. Here are nine areas that are the greatest hindrances to our worship. Scripture references serve as prescriptions that bring deliverance and healing in these areas of your life. Apply God's Word now, so your worship experience can no longer be hindered by you. God wants you to be free to worship Him in Spirit and Truth.

1. Pride

2. Feeling Unworthy / Guilt and Condemnation

3. Unforgiveness

4. Mind Elsewhere / Distracted

5. The Devil – Wants our Worship

6. Emotions Feelings

7. Religious Traditions

8. Sentimentalism

9. Lips

10. Heart

11. Fear of Manipulation

1) *Pride*

Proverbs 11:2
When pride comes, then comes disgrace, but with humility comes wisdom.

Pride (disambiguation) is a high sense of the worth of one's self and one's own, or a pleasure taken in the contemplation of these things. (Wikipedia, the free encyclopedia)

2) *Feeling Unworthy / Guilt and Condemnation*

1 Chronicles 21:8
"Then David said to God, "I have sinned greatly by doing this. Now, I beg you, take away the guilt of your servant. I have done a very foolish thing."

Ps.103:12
as far as the east is from the west, so far has he removed our transgressions from us.

Rom 8:1-2
Therefore, there is now no condemnation for those who are in Christ Jesus, ² because through Christ Jesus the law of the Spirit of life set me free from the law of sin and death.

Come before God and allow Him to convict you of sin. He will convict but not condemn us. Conviction will lead us to repentance, condemnation to despair (John 3:17, 8:11). Draw as near to God as you possibly can. Run to His presence and confess your sins and receive His cleansing, healing, holiness, and purity.

3. *Unforgiveness*

Eph. 4:31-32
Get rid of all bitterness, rage and anger, brawling and slander, along with every form of malice. ³² Be kind and compassionate to one another, forgiving each other, just as in Christ God forgave you.

Heb 12:15

See to it that no one comes short of the grace of God; that no root of bitterness springing up causes trouble, and by it may be defiled;

Forgiveness is ALWAYS costly! But the cost of forgiving others is nothing compared to God forgiving us or the price that He paid for us - His own humiliation, torture, and death on the cross!

4.   *When your MIND is Elsewhere or DISTRACTED*

2 Corn. 10:5

We demolish arguments and every pretension that sets itself up against the knowledge of God, and we take captive every thought to make it obedient to Christ.

We are, by nature, sinful, and if we live by our nature, we will not get close to God. That is why we need to die to ourselves, and live in Christ (Romans 6:11). But no matter what we do, there will always be a constant battle within ourselves between our spirit and our flesh (Romans 7:15-21). That is why we need to constantly allow God to search our heart and purify it (Psalm 139:23-24).

It is a constant struggle to keep our eyes fixed on Jesus without becoming distracted by the passing concerns and things of this world such as money, finances, media, relationships, church, work, hobbies, etc. But, if we are aware of what can, and does, interfere with our walks with God, we can begin to take the necessary actions to prevent them.

5.   *The Devil – He Wants our Worship*

<u>John 10:10</u>
The thief comes only to steal and kill and destroy; I have come that they may have life, and have it to the full.

<u>1st Peter 5:8</u>
Be alert and of sober mind. Your enemy the devil prowls around like a roaring lion looking for someone to devour.

Your adversary is not someone who made you upset, nor the person who cut in front of your car on your way to church. It is not the person who arrives late for church every Sunday and creates a scene trying to find a seat on your row. Your adversary is the devil. Do not allow the enemy to steal your praise.

6.   *Emotions / Feelings*

<u>Matt 26:41</u>
"Watch and pray so that you will not fall into temptation. The spirit is willing, but the flesh is weak."

<u>Romans 7:22-23</u>
For in my inner being I delight in God's law; [23] but I see another law at work in me, waging war against the law of my mind and making me a prisoner of the law of sin at work within me.

If we allow our worship to be controlled by our feelings, we will never gain victory in our Christian walk. We don't worship because we feel like it. Worship brings us into the presence of God. If we do not enter into the presence of God, we cannot grow spiritually, therefore we die spiritually.

7. *Religious Tradition*

> <u>Mark 7:3, 5, -9</u>
> [3] *(The Pharisees and all the Jews do not eat unless they give their hands a ceremonial washing, holding to the tradition of the elders. ...[5] So the Pharisees and teachers of the law asked Jesus, "Why don't your disciples live according to the tradition of the elders instead of eating their food with defiled hands?" ..."These people honor me with their lips, but their hearts are far from me. [7] They worship me in vain; their teachings are merely human rules.' [8] You have let go of the commands of God and are holding on to human traditions." [9]..."You have a fine way of setting aside the commands of God in order to observe your own traditions!*

Religions and Christianity have numerous traditions. There were certain experiences God did instruct us to repeat over and over again. But His Word becomes ineffective when overshadowed by Religious traditions. We should keep our spiritual eyes and ears open to the things of God and never allow our worship to become a tradition.

8. *Sentimentalism*

> <u>Song of Songs 1:15-16</u>
> *(He) How beautiful you are, my darling! Oh, how beautiful! Your eyes are doves. (She)16 How handsome you are, my beloved! Oh, how charming! And our bed is verdant.*

Sentimentalism is defined as an expression of tender emotional memories of special events, music, and other significant things; excessive indulgences; mushy, (Collins English Dictionary - Complete & Unabridged 10th Edition).

Sentimentalism is like salt. Too much ruins the dish. We often become sentimental in worship when we become more taken up with the music or tune than with the message of the song. Overly familiar songs are in danger of becoming sentimental for us. We should not just respond emotionally, instead we need a complete response of our whole beings. Music should help us open our hearts and become more receptive to Him rather than worship the music.

9. *Lips*

<u>Proverbs 10:13-14</u>
Wisdom is found on the lips of the discerning, but a rod is for the back of one who has no sense. [14] The wise store up knowledge, but the mouth of a fool invites ruin.

James 3:3-6
[3] *When we put bits into the mouths of horses to make them obey us, we can turn the whole animal. [4] Or take ships as an example. Although they are so large and are driven by strong winds, they are steered by a very small rudder wherever the pilot wants to go. [5] Likewise, the tongue is a small part of the body, but it makes great boasts. Consider what a great forest is set on fire by a small spark. [6] The tongue also is a fire, a world of evil among the parts of the body. It corrupts the whole body, sets the whole course of one's life on fire, and is itself set on fire by hell.*

James illustrates the power of the tongue using metaphors.
a) He likens the tongue to the bits we put in horses mouths. We can control a 2,000-pound horse with a small bit in his mouth.

b) He likens the tongue to the rudder of a ship. A huge ship can be steered in any direction with a relatively small rudder. James' point in these metaphors is that the tongue is a small part of our body.

Because it is so small, we might think it is rather inconsequential. We might think the words we speak are really no big deal. But James is telling us to think again. Our words can set the whole direction of our lives.

10. *Heart - Your Heart can be a Hindrance in Worship*

1 Samuel 16:7
But the Lord said to Samuel, "Do not consider his appearance or his height, for I have rejected him. The Lord does not look at the things people look at. People look at the outward appearance, but the Lord looks at the heart."

Ps. 19:14
Let the words of my mouth, and the meditation of my heart, be acceptable in thy sight, O LORD, my strength, and my redeemer.

Prov. 4:23
Above all else, guard your heart, for it is the wellspring of life.

Why is the heart so important? Why does it need to be guarded with such diligence? The word heart is found 963 times in the Bible. Of these usages, the heart can mean the mind, the emotions, the will, or the inner man. It can even refer to the person as a whole.

The heart is important because it conceives life. Think of the heart as being the womb where all of our actions, attitudes, ambitions and articulations are conceived. So the things we do are a product of the heart. Our words spoken are evidence of what lies within our heart.

11. *Fear of Manipulation*

<u>John 16:13</u>
When he, the Spirit of truth, comes, he will guide you into all truth.

<u>Psa. 116:6</u>
The Lord protects the simple hearted; when I was in great need, he saved me.

The Holy Spirit protects us from manipulators of scripture by teaching us to how to discern truth; knowing right from wrong, and seeing manipulative tricks of the enemy. We must fear God not man. The Lord fights the battles for those who lack knowledge, wisdom, and understanding.

Let us lay aside all those inward sins and things that will hinder our worship from reaching God, so we can experience His presence. We want Him to accept our praise and worship. I pray that we would come to worship ready to give to God with a true heart of repentance, for the heart does not lie.

Chapter 7

MIND CHANGING EVENTS

I will love the light for it shows me the way,
yet I will endure the darkness for it shows me the stars.
- Og Mandino

June 2010 was a year of events that quickly changed my life. First I began experiencing excruciating headaches that I tried to ignore. One day I finally decided to take some pain medicine. I was hoping the headaches would cease, but there was never a total relief. Then I traveled to St. Kitts in the Caribbean to minister at a worship conference. One night I experienced an excruciating headache that caused teary eyes while standing onstage in the presence of florescent lights. It was so annoying until I had to position myself where I could avoid those lights.

On June 26th, 2010, while in the St. Kitts airport preparing to return to Nassau, Bahamas, I purchased both Excedrin and Aspirin hoping to get some relief from the constant headache. Within the next four hours, I had taken at least three or four of each pill but neither gave me any relief. I boarded the airplane perspiring so much until one of the stewardesses noticed it. She checked on me a few times after I was seated; I was constantly asked whether everything was okay. After a few inquiries, I finally told her I had a headache and she asked if I wanted something. I informed her that I had already taken something.

MOVE OVER EGO

There was some relief in my mind when the airplane finally landed and I was headed home. The headaches continued causing me to stay awake through the night, so I decided to get up and prepare breakfast for my family. My wife Cyprianna looked at me and noticed something strange. She could not say what it was except that I had been acting different since I returned from St. Kitts. My Christian response was "So if that's the case, pray for me." My ego was not accepting her observation, and neither was I accepting my physical symptoms.

The following day was a Sunday and attending church was a routine part of my life. After all I was the worship leader and director of the Fine Arts Department at Bahamas Faith Ministries International here in Nassau, Bahamas. Our entire Service is watched around the world through internet television streaming. Unfortunately my doctor did not release me to return to my church duties. Also, I was still sleeping a lot from being heavily medicated. So I had to stay home, which was most unusual.

One of my routine Sunday commitments was extending a ride to a couple who lives nearby. I forgot to call and let them know I wasn't going to church, so I decided to drive to their home and see if they still needed a ride. If so, I would take them and come directly back home to rest. When I arrived at their home, I parked my car in their driveway and sat listening to the radio until I fell asleep for at least three hours before returning home. Another big surprise came when I entered my front door and was greeted by my family. I discovered they had already returned from church. My wife asked if I had visited another church. I told her that I went to pick up the couple who rides with me, but they weren't home. She said they were in church. One of my daughters heard our conversation and said she forgot to inform me that the couple had called on the previous day stating they would be riding to church with someone else.

Sunday afternoon was passing and those excruciating headaches showed no sign of relief, which led me to call a family friend who is a nurse. I told her about my headaches and sought advice on what to do. She came immediately to check my blood pressure and it was extremely elevated. Her boss is a cardiologist, so she contacted to get further advice concerning my blood pressure and headaches. The cardiologist said I should go to the hospital emergency room for immediate medical attention. I followed his instructions and went to the emergency room at Doctor's Hospital where a CAT scan was completed to see what was happening inside my head. The results showed some bleeding and a big mass of blood that needed to be removed in order to stop the bleeding. That was the last thing I remembered due to an injection that put me to sleep so the doctors could perform the surgery.

"DO NOT TOUCH"

The removal of a portion of my skull caused the discovery of a tumor on my brain. The medical team proceeded in removing two-thirds of the tumor to make sure that it was not cancerous. I did not wake up until the following morning yet to another surprise.

Placing my hand on my head whenever I wake up has been a habit and I was about to do that, but the doctor stopped me as he said: "You must not touch your head because it contains some stitches." My shocking response was "stitches?" He replied, "Yeah, we had to do an immediate surgery on your head last night. Do not touch your head because it is swollen and we had to remove a part of your skull. That portion of your brain is semi-exposed, so just leave it alone." Curiosity made me want to see what my head looked like, so I got up and headed straight to the bathroom mirror. I did not recognize the person I saw in the mirror; my head was swollen quite large. God and I had a talk immediately after taking a look in the mirror. I told Him I did not know what that was all about but I was placing all my trust in Him; my life was

His hands. Every day I woke up thanking God for the healing of my head to quickly manifest.

I recall each time the doctor came to examine me, he would say, "I don't understand this but everything is coming together so quickly." I did not tell him how I was praying. A month later I returned to the hospital as an outpatient to have the stitches removed from my head. When the doctor saw me again, he said, "Oh my God!" My response was "no, He's my God." I was not sure whether the doctor was a Christian until he responded, "I know what you are saying." He was pleased with my progress.

IT'S TIME TO SING AGAIN

Thirty-two staples were used to close my head until I returned another four weeks later to have the remainder of the tumor removed from my brain. My healing was becoming evident. I thought there would be no more surgeries. Days went by without any seizures or physical challenges. In my mind, there was enough evidence to let me know I could return to church and be a part of the worship team.

Bahamas Faith Ministries was celebrating thirty (30) years of ministry in August 2010, so I decided to join the worship team in our Sunday morning Anniversary Celebration. In my mind, I just knew it was time for me to sing again. I felt excited and ready to step back onstage with a microphone. The Sunday morning praise and worship was awesome and I was happy to be back onstage leading worship. The event would conclude that Sunday night, so I rushed home after church to have lunch and return to lead worship again. I did not recall feeling bad while onstage during the evening service, but at some point I fainted while singing. The medical doctors and nurses who attend BFM came to my rescue. They worked hard to revive me after my heart had stopped four times.

IS THE SONG FINISHED?

The hospital was not a place where I wanted to find myself again; neither did I want to believe my body had six broken ribs that occurred during four rounds of CPR. Being there again could only be in a dream.

On the following morning I remembered being awakened by a nurse. That was quite a surprise. I heard her say, "Pastor Mark! You need to get up. You've slept a long time." My first response was, "Is the song finished?" She replied, "Your song? You're in the hospital." I asked, "How did I get here." She said, "You were transported by an ambulance after having four heart attacks. So the doctor needs to examine you to find out what is going on. We need to make sure there aren't any other problems." The joke was on me since I woke up from the coma on the following morning thinking that I was still leading Sunday night worship. After all, it was the last thing I was doing before I fainted.

When I was released from the hospital, the doctor said I would have a twelve (12) week recovery period. During that time I underwent therapy although my brain was not experiencing any deficits; no malfunctions. The therapy was to ensure that everything was in good order. I had four appointments with the doctor and each time he said I was having a speedy recovery. So I told him I did not need any therapy because I was okay. Then the Holy Spirit reminded me that I also thought I was okay when my body was sending signals of headaches that were letting me know all was not well.

Soon I returned to work not long after being released from the hospital. Perhaps it was too soon. The evidence came one day while at work when I had a seizure alone in my office. That was not the first time; I had already encountered a seizure in my office one Sunday night shortly before a Christmas concert began in my honor on December 18, 2011. It happened shortly before the program began when I had gone to my office to get the words to a song for someone. Thank God another person was with me to call for help. I was taken to the hospital to be examined while other members of my family went up to receive the honor on my behalf. I was later able to watch the event on a DVD.

RECALIBRATING

When I met with my doctor, I shared some concerns about the seizures. I wanted to know how long it would take for my recovery. That's when I learned more about the brain and how it functions in the healing process. The doctor explained that it would be impossible to know the exact length of time it would take for my healing, because my brain was recalibrating after being normal for over fifty (50) years - my age. It needed to recalibrate but the scar tissue was being recognized as a foreign object that caused the seizures.

"MIND CHANGING"

Experiencing this extensive medical condition has also allowed me to discover a new kind of worship; one that I never knew existed. Finding it under these conditions is my deepest regret. But, this experience has helped in my preparation for true worship. I've discovered that true worship requires spending quality time in the King's Court. It is a special place that I find difficult to describe. Being able to worship God all over again can best be expressed through the phrase "mind changing."

These past few months have been a time of carefully observing the power of God moving in my life in ways that I do not understand; neither can I explain them. My best description is that everything I previously did in preparation for worship has become history. I feel compelled to worship God like it is my first time ever entering His presence. The old way is just not adequate for Who He is and what He has done for me. My presence on this earth is because of His grace and mercy that says I still have more to contribute that will bring glory to God's kingdom on earth.

We must know who we are worshipping and whether our worship is real. Each of the four times that I awakened from a coma, I totally surrendered everything that was left within me - whatever God was preserving. Unfortunately it took this long for me to realize everything that I have left is HIS; my worship is based only on His terms. I am talking about twenty-five (25) years since my spiritual birth, which shows how much we can become used to worship like a habit.

This new mind changing worship experience is coming through a deep personal relationship that speaks to the ONE who deserves it. My focus has shifted from singing songs - to studying God so I can know how to please Him. It does not mean my worship was previously carnal minded. Sometimes my flesh did prevail and my singing became commercialized. But I have learned that a carnal mind can definitely hinder the flow of spiritual substance in our worship.

Worship alone with God has become very special. I want to remain in His presence where I am experiencing a new and refreshing fullness of joy. This is the place where the psalmist David says God makes known our path of life; He fills us with joy in His presence and eternal pleasures at His hand (Psalm 16:11).

Chapter 8

A NEW REVELATION
ABOUT WORSHIP

God, the object of our worship, also becomes
the inspiration of that worship. He has imparted His own
Spirit into our hearts to energize that worship.
All that is due Him comes from Him.
- Judson Cornwall

I have been studying God's design pattern that was established when He created the world. In the Bible, Genesis chapter one describes how God created me in His image and His likeness, which means I embody His nature and character. Whenever God spoke, it was powerful. His words were spoken with dynamism and they were designed to impact future generations.

GENERATIONAL FREQUENCIES

God designed Creation in frequencies. The New Miriam Webster Dictionary defines a *frequency* as:

1. The fact or condition of occurring frequently;

2. The number of times that a periodic function repeats the same sequence of values during a unit variation of the independent variable;

3. The number, proportion, or percentage of items in a particular category in a set of data.

Understanding a frequency in Creation has been a like a light switch turned on in my head. When God said, "*Let there be light,*" that was a *frequency*, which went from generation to generation. Light was only created one time, but we see daylight every day. God called forth day and night, evening and morning.

Genesis 1:3-5
And God said, "Let there be light," and there was light. ⁴ God saw that the light was good, and he separated the light from the darkness. ⁵ God called the light "day," and the darkness he called "night." And there was evening, and there was morning- the first day.

One day while mowing my front lawn, I stopped to pull up some weeds. Two days later it rained and I soon found more weeds popping up in the same area. The Holy Spirit showed me how that was a frequency moving through generations. To further understand the frequency process, I called my friend Pastor Pepe Ramnath, a scientist (Mira Mar, Florida), and he was able to help me understand it. The Holy Spirit was showing me the "frequency" in many things on earth, but the frequency in praise and worship stood out.

THE PRAISE OF OUR WORSHIP

God has placed the praise of our worship in us so we can share it with others. He alone releases the glory. This revelation came when I thought about the biblical story of Jesus' triumphant entrance into the city of Jerusalem on Palm Sunday. He arrived on a donkey and observed the children, the shouting, and waving of palm branches that were laid along the road. The people were shouting "*Blessed is he who comes in the name of the Lord.*" The Pharisees tried to stop their praise, but Jesus responded by saying "*I tell you,*" he replied, "*if they keep quiet, the stones will cry out*" (Luke 19:40).

The Holy Spirit showed me how praise was a frequency originating from Creation. Whatever God says in the beginning continues through all generations. He designed everything needed in our frequencies once and for all. There was no need for Him to go back and add something else to His divine plan for mankind. God uses the same frequency that He spoke in the beginning. Within me is the ability to do the same thing. We are to speak those things that are not as though they exist (Romans 4:17). Whenever I hear my wife and daughters say they cannot find something that they misplaced, I tell them to stop speaking the negative. Instead they need to call that thing by its name; there is a frequency. God established a law of attraction connected to that frequency.

FREQUENCY PRINCIPLES

The last time I was hospitalized my doctor and his medical team expected me to be there for a longer time period. They were not aware of my morning ritual of speaking to my head. I would touch my head and address it with these words: *By His stripes I am healed. I speak to every tissue and cell and I command them to take their rightful place.* God wants us to apply the same frequency principle to our worship, because He wants to manifest His presence in our lives. Here are a few frequency principles:

1) *God will never turn his back on us.*

    Matthew 28:20
    Teaching them to observe all things whatsoever I have commanded you: and, lo, I am with you always, even unto the end of the world. Amen.

Last night the Holy Spirit reminded me that the Lord will never leave me or forsake me. Sometimes we overlook that in our worship. God is an ever present help in our time of troubles. We say it and it sounds good, but I do not believe we have allowed those words to penetrate the depth of our heart. There the Holy Spirit showed me another frequency at work, because God never turns His back on us. He is always with us.

A few days later I went to the hospital for a check-up and saw one of the nurses who used to sit and chat with me at night. She said, "Man you look so good. You made it through the battle really great."

I responded, "Please don't think I'm being forward with this, but I know that." She said "No, no I don't think so. You know one of the things that encouraged me when you were in hospital was that every time we came to your room and asked how you were doing, your response was that you were doing great. I captured that and began to apply it to my life. Since you were first hospitalized two years ago, my life has changed." I responded, "That's the law of attraction at work. You must create your own environment." When I was being discharged from the hospital, she said, "Alright take…" as in take care. But she remembered what I had taught her and her sentence changed to "No, not *take*, you *cast* your cares."

This illness has definitely helped me to understand that being a worship leader positions me to have a broad influence on people. Sometimes there is hardly any noticeable measurement in life. Now I am able to see results. Lives are being transformed and my heart is encouraged.

I recently learned that many worship leaders and people who know me have been talking about some of the things that I taught them over the years. They are sharing how their language has changed causing them to speak the right words over their circumstances. Some have said they see the positive effects upon their life. Their testimonies have encouraged me. I realize they were receiving more than what came through the songs I sang during praise and worship.

2) *He will never leave us or forsake us.*

Joshua 1:5
No one will be able to stand against you all the days of your life. As I was with Moses, so I will be with you; I will never leave you nor forsake you.

Last night I thought about God's love for us and how HE will never leave us nor forsake us. Then I heard the Spirit say, "*Be courageous Mark for I will never leave you.*" Those words were a constant reminder while hospitalized. When the doctor would ask me how I was doing, I would tell him I was doing well and he would ask whether I was sure. My response was a sign of being courageous. I was not paying attention to what that doctor thought about me, it is God who does the healing.

3) *God inhales our worship and He exhales His glory!*

The Word says that God inhabits the praises of His people (Psalm 22:3). It's amazing to think that God, in all His fullness, inhales our worship. He exhales whatever is needed to make a situation turn around for the good. If you could grasp this truth, you would understand that every time you worship Him, He is present to meet your needs.

We must never underestimate the effect of our worship upon God's heart. As soon as He hears us call His name, He is ready to answer us. Every time we worship Him, His presence comes.

Psalm 8:2
From the lips of children and infants you have ordained praise because of your enemies, to silence the foe and the avenger.

The psalmist tells us that even our babies have been ordained by the Lord Most High to silence the enemy with praise. When you sing, praise, dance, and rejoice in the face of opposition, you are using the spiritual warfare weapons against the devil. He is exalted above anything that you face — above any disappointment, above any brokenness, above anything that tries to exalt itself higher than the name of Jesus. He has promised us His Name and His Word.

4)   *God lives in our praise but not our problems.*

One day I was sitting in my family room thinking about some financial commitments that needed to be met at that time. It occurred to me that I needed to attract the presence of God instead of focusing on our finances. God lives in our praise not in our problems. He lives in our worship but not in our problems.

I began worshipping the Lord in a normal voice when suddenly it became loud. Later I heard the telephone ringing; it was someone at the office calling to let me know that I had some mail, which she had accidently opened. She saw a check inside and wanted to know what I wanted her to do with it. I told her to give it to my administrative assistant and I would collect it on the following day. After I hung up the phone I felt led to go immediately to the office rather than wait until the next day. When I received the envelope, the first thing I noticed was its postmark from Australia, a place I had never visited neither did I know anyone there. Attached to the back of the letter was a check. The letter said, "Dear Pastor Mark: You have blessed us for so many years and we just wanted to bless you, so we are sending this check to you." When I saw the amount on the check, there was another level of worship that took place within me. It was more than our financial commitments.

5) *We work our faith but God works His glory.*

Matthew 9:29
Then he touched their eyes and said, "According to your faith let it be done to you";

Isaiah 48:11
For my own sake, for my own sake, I do this. How can I let myself be defamed? I will not yield my glory to another.

Our faith must be exercised if we want to see God's glory. He determines if and when he's going to show up. While driving home after receiving that letter and check as far away as Australia, I realized the need to keep working my faith so God can work His glory.

My revelation knowledge about God's design pattern is comforting in knowing that He created frequency patterns in worship to meet all my needs. I was on His mind when He designed frequency patterns for never turning His back on me, never leaving me, being with me always, inhaling my worship and exhaling His glory, living in my praise not my problem, making provisions for my healing and faith to operate, while He works His Glory. What an awesome revelation about God that has and forever will impact future generations.

Chapter 9

MY SEASON OF
PREPARATION

*The beginning of the good news about Jesus the Messiah, the
Son of God, ² as it is written in Isaiah the prophet: "I will send
my messenger ahead of you, who will prepare your way" ³"a voice
of one calling in the wilderness, 'Prepare the way for the Lord,
make straight paths for him."*
- Mark 1:1-3

There is nothing like the fullness of joy that comes with being able to properly prepare for worship with Almighty God. It is a place that I did not know could exist. I have no words to describe the sweet commune I am experiencing in the presence of my heavenly Father.

Preparation is a key element to worshipping God, which required some corrections within me. Over the years I have done many things in my worship that had no substance. When I started leading worship at church, I wanted my senior pastor, Dr. Myles Munroe, to teach me since I was previously a gospel singer. I was used to being on stage and performing at concerts where people left the same way they came; some in wheelchairs and some crippled on the inside.

Becoming a worship leader was my ultimate reason for learning how to enter God's presence. I needed to see what it could do for people. Singing was my natural gift and I had good eye contact, but I needed to see the end result of worship.

I've learned that true worship requires preparation. I wonder how many people enjoy the work that goes into a finished product. Mark 1:2 says there is a time of preparation before the reality of anticipation, before the appearance of the Lord Jesus Christ. In Exodus 23:20, God sent an angel ahead of the children of Israel to prepare the way for them to enter their Promised Land.

PREPARATION PRINCIPLES

1)   *You are in the preparation mode now.*

Everything you do today is in preparation for tomorrow. Preparation is a daily thing not a destination. Fighters do not become champions in the ring. They are merely recognized in the ring. Their becoming happens in their daily routine. Our only preparation for tomorrow is the right use of today.

> *You can map out a fight plan or a life plan.*
> *But when the action starts, you're down to your reflexes.*
> *That's where your roadwork shows.*
> *If you cheated on that in the dark of the morning,*
> *you're getting found out now under the bright lights.*
> - Joe Frazier (*Wikipedia, Frazier, Joe*)

2)   *Preparing prevents repairing.*

Preparation far exceeds the amount of time that you are actually in a performance but preparing takes even longer. Ask a carpenter and you will learn that it is better to measure twice and have to saw only once.

3) *Preparation today brings confidence and success for tomorrow.*

The time to prepare the roof is when the sun is shining.
- (Wikipedia, JFK)

Preparation begins with knowing what you want, so you can know where to go and how to find the right people; ask the right questions; and pay the right price.

4) *Preparation requires quality time and commitment to the assignment.*

Some worship leaders would rather be in a worship service than preparing for it. After all, enjoying a relaxing vacation is much better than the preparation and time needed to reach your destination.

Once I was returning to Nassau by plane thinking we were about to land because of our close proximity to the airport. The plane's wheels were ready to touch down when I realized the aircraft was gaining altitude. The pilot immediately addressed us saying, "I know you are wondering why we went back up. It was because we were informed that the ground crew was not ready for us." They needed more time for the preparation that involved coordination of ground crew and those inside the terminal. Peeping through the small window I saw the ground crew moving swiftly to get things in place for our plane to dock. Then the Holy Spirit revealed to me that the pilot needed permission for the plane to be received. The thought entered my mind about worship and how much preparation is made for our worship to be received by God.

My season of preparation is requiring me to be still before God. It fits well with being away from the workplace and working at home. My brain is still recalibrating and I have to remind myself that it is not an overnight process. Our Fine Arts Department has a wonderful leadership team and we are in communication on a daily basis.

Working from home and participating in our church services through the internet streaming has many wonderful benefits. My intimate time with God allows me to enter into the kind of worship that I know will bring glory to Him. When I enter His presence and He begins to release His glory, I want to benefit from it.

SIGNS OF PREPARATION

Sitting in the pews on Sunday mornings allows me to observe whether adequate preparation was made for the entrance of God's holy presence. The Holy Spirit has shown me three key principles about signs of preparation for his holy entrance:

1. If there are no signs of preparation, God will not show up.

2. God's presence will never show up where He is not invited.

3. If our preparation is not for God, then we are only going through religious calisthenics; it is a waste of energy.

My medical situation has forced me to think about what I bring to the Lord and how I present it to Him. It cannot happen through talking or singing, but acknowledging that everything about my living belongs to God. The air that I breathe belongs to Him. That alone makes me realize how much I need Him. My breathing cannot happen on my own terms. I must approach God on His terms and understand what He requires for me to enter His presence.

RIGHT THINKING – RIGHT FOOD

Experiencing God now is different from how I perceived Him before having the heart attacks. He always backs up HIS Word! It is His oath; He cannot and will not lie. Therefore, I make a conscious effort to speak words that feed my spirit because they enhance my entire being. Right thinking is the right food that lines up with the word of God. I am required to stay calm, rest, and avoid arguments or discussions, especially about unfamiliar topics. This requires me to keep the right thoughts in my head.

I am learning how to feed my brain the right food. For instance, it is good to know God's word brings healing. Sometimes people will say "Take care" as they are leaving my house, but I remind them that we are to cast our cares rather than take it. We carry too many cares and anxieties that we cannot handle, and God's word says that we should cast them on Him, because He cares for us (I Peter 5:7).

This special diet of right thinking is allowing me to observe some things in worship for the first time ever. They are difficult to share, but I've tried sharing some with my wife. I have learned to be careful in choosing words that come from my mouth, because they determine the environment that I create for God. I can choose to look at situations and circumstances and speak the wrong words, and say things that do not represent Him. It is a choice and I constantly remind myself that my thoughts and words need to emulate God.

No matter how many sophisticated ideas come about worship, the burning thing in my heart is that I am where God wants me to be. When He laid out his instructions to Moses, they were precise in every way. There was a picture and a pattern of how He wanted us to come to Him. Unfortunately we do not always see those elements and that is how we head in the wrong direction.

You may be wondering why I am repeating myself when sharing how much I want my worship to matter to God. Living and breathing is good, but my eyes are filled with tears because there are times when I really do not need to be here.

When I think about the first day I was hospitalized, I learned that a friend, who is also a worship leader, was hospitalized with a similar medical diagnosis. Unfortunately, he did not recover and went to be with the Lord. But God allowed my heart to beat again and again after stopping four times. That is enough to bring tears to my eyes and make me want to worship Him like never before. My motivation is that God has preserved me. I am talking about the One who knew me before I was born so I could have the opportunity to know Him. There must be a reason for my existence since He has kept me thus far. So right thinking has helped me in keeping things in the proper perspective.

Years ago I participated in a worship conference in England where one of the sessions addressed the word "thanksgiving," which is an old English derivative from "to think." It means we should enter God's presence with think-giving rather than thanksgiving. The implication is that we need to think about what we are bringing to the Lord. He wants us to present our offering as a willing sacrifice to the fullest extent and in a respectable manner.

Psalms 100 says we must enter His gates with thanksgiving. We must not be guided by popular clichés and catchy phrases to bring pure worship before God. None of that matters to Him. I can say this with the utmost sincerity after having gone through two brain surgeries, four heart attacks, and six broken ribs. That is why I believe we must enter His gates with think-giving.

Thinking about God's unconditional love for me is overwhelming. There are no words to describe how grateful I am for His goodness, His grace, and everything that He has brought me through since the beginning of my illness in June 2010. Every day I wake up feeling compelled to give thanks. I have no choice.

TOTAL SURRENDER

"The greatness of a man's power is the measure of his surrender."
- William Booth

This is a brand new season for me. It is no longer about what or how I did things in the past. I am in a place of total surrender to God. Old things have passed away and HE has made all things new to me. God is so awesome, I feel like I am just beginning to understand true worship and what is required to engage His presence. God is my ever present help and I'm chasing Him like it's my first time.

Conclusion

PURPOSE FULFILLED, MISSION ACCOMPLISHED, DESTINY ACHIEVED

In June 2010, Pastor Dr. Mark Anthony Bethel would begin a road of medical challenges which culminated on July 11, 2012, when this Distinguished Kingdom Ambassador was recalled.

Pastor Mark was a worship leader par excellence. He had the distinct honor and an uncanny ability to lead people into the presence of God, an assignment to which he wholly committed himself. He had a passion for music and the role it plays in worship. Mark also had the ability to envision and energize a worship community that is grounded in the great hymns of the past and the current expressions of worship, while embracing the original songs emerging from the prophets and minstrels. He was sensitive to and respected the prophetic flow and ensured that his worship enhanced it.

Mark was a leader with a deep love for the Lord Jesus Christ and His people. He believed that an effective worship leader is first and foremost a worshipper. Mark believed the best way to lead others in worship is to worship God yourself; that we must be filled to overflowing with the Holy Spirit so we can minister to others out of that "overflow." To this end, he gave himself to prayer, meditation, and the study of God's Word – the closer our relationship with God, the deeper our worship will be.

It was at Bahamas Faith Ministries International (BFMI) that Pastor Mark would be given a platform for his ministry. He served along with Senior Pastor Dr. Myles Munroe as a member of the Praise and Worship Team, which he would eventually lead and go on to develop into a Fine Arts Ministry. On becoming members of BFMI in 1980, Mark and his family became fully engaged in all aspects of the life of the Church. In addition to worship, he also managed the Church's bookstore, served as director of the pre-school and as a pastor. For his outstanding contribution to BFMI, he received the Lifetime Achievement award on December 18, 2012. Pastor Mark was awarded an honorary Doctorate of Divinity degree on April 15, 2012.

Dr. Mark Bethel was most internationally recognized for his contribution to kingdom-building as an extraordinary worship leader. The first indication of his tremendous talent was through his transformation of young minds in the classroom, which would represent a significant contribution to nation-building. He began his career as an educator in 1973 as an untrained teacher at Western Senior School. He received his formal training as an educator at the Bahamas Teachers' College, and graduated with a Teacher's Certificate in 1976. He received a Bachelor of Science in Education from the University of Miami in 1978. Throughout his distinguished career, he taught at primary and secondary schools, both private and public, including Claridge Primary, C. I. Gibson Junior High, Temple Christian School, and Seed Life School.

Mark would also move through ranks from Untrained Teacher to Vice Principal to Director. His work as an educator contributed to the development of many disciplined, focused citizens who now serve this nation and the international community with distinction. His contribution to the development of the youth was not limited to their intellect and character, but extended to the physical needs. He used skills as a premier athlete to enhance the development of physical education programs in the primary schools in addition to assisting students with special needs.

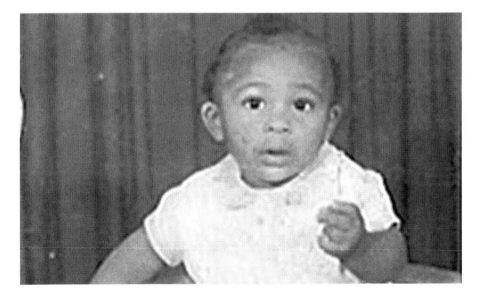

Who would imagine that the boy-child born to the union of William Salathiel and Ethlyn Mae Bethel on the glorious morning of October 17, 1955, would go on to change the manner of worship in this nation, The Bahamas. He would be called Mark Anthony.

From childhood, it was evident that this child was gifted both athletically and vocally. He was extremely agile and came alive at the sound of music and singing. His prowess on the basketball court gave him the name "Bumble." These skills would be equally demonstrated as he sprinted down the track for his beloved A. F. Adderley High School where he had the distinction of serving as Head Boy.

Mark would not let his athletic ability out shine his music. It was very early in his adult life that he galvanized his friends around the formation of the famous "Love Singers." From this group emerged the national gospel hit "The Christian ABC." Later Mark immersed himself into praise and worship. This minstrel became a minister of music, who ministered with excellence, both nationally and internationally including the Caribbean, the USA, Europe, Canada and the Islands of The Bahamas.

Mark was affectionate and compassionate, he loved family. When he married Cyprianna Johnson in 1977, he could not fathom how this mystical union would strengthen and enhance his gifting. "Cypri" would prove to be the God-ordained help mate that would inspire and support his efforts, providing a home-base that nourished his body and soul. This union brought forth three incredible daughters, each embodying some of his many gifting and graces from education, to music, to athletics. Although Mark was the biological father of three daughters: Tamara, Tonya and Amari, many adopted daughters called him "Paps," "Dad" or "Daddy." He was a father to the fatherless and an uncle to many sons. Mark treasured family and was always ready to have a family gathering. He made no distinction between his family and friends. Mark was a peacemaker and a good listener, a family man who promoted family harmony and unity. He was small in his own eyes but had a big heart.

ALWAYS SANCTIFIED
ALWAYS PRAISING HIM

All the Levites who were musicians - Asaph, Heman, Jeduthun and their sons and relatives - stood on the east side of the altar, dressed in fine linen and playing cymbals, harps and lyres.
They were accompanied by 120 priests sounding trumpets.
[13] The trumpeters and musicians joined in unison to give praise and thanks to the LORD. Accompanied by trumpets, cymbals and other instruments, the singers raised their voices in praise to the LORD and sang:
"He is good; his love endures forever."
Then the temple of the LORD was filled with the cloud,
[14] and the priests could not perform their service because of the cloud, for the glory of the LORD filled the temple of God.
- 2 Chronicles 5:12-14

This distinguished worship leader embodied all the qualities of a Levite:

- He was joined to the Lord Jesus Christ, committed to pastoral leadership, and he embraced the vision of the local church.

- He had a servant's heart and lived a sanctified lifestyle that exhibited a spirit of forgiveness, a heart of loyalty, and a willingness to serve.

- He was trustworthy and an example to others as he inspired them to desire the same depth of relationship with the Lord that he enjoyed.

- He was a man of integrity, consistency and steadfastness; one who always did the right thing regardless of the cost.

- Generous and selfless, he always put others before himself.

- He was passionate, energetic, committed, focused and humorous.

- He lived a life of praise, worship, and thanksgiving, which gave birth to ASAPH as a training forum for fine arts and worship leaders to join him at the Diplomat Center in Nassau, Bahamas:

"Always Sanctified, Always Praising Him."

Appendix

FAMILY
TRIBUTES

Cyprianna Bethel

Markie,

Dear Husband In Heaven
I sit here and I ponder how very much
I'd like to talk to you today.
There are so many things
That we didn't get to say.
I know how much you care for me
And how much I care for you,
And each time that I think of you
I know you'll miss me too.
An angel came and called your name
And took you by the hand and said
Your place was ready in Heaven, far above…
And you have to leave behind, all those you dearly loved
You had so much to live for; you had so much to do…
It still seemed impossible, that God was taking you.
And though your life on earth is past, in Heaven it starts anew
You'll live for all eternity, just as God has promised you.
And though you've walked through Heaven's gate
We are never far apart
For each time that we think of you,
You're right here, deep with-in our hearts.

Cypri

TAmara Bethel

Thinking About You...

As I sit and think... I find myself wondering...
Did I remember to thank you enough for all you did for me?
For all the times you were by my side to help and support me
...to celebrate my successes, understand my problems
and accept my defeat?
For teaching me by example, the value of hard work,
good judgment, courage, and integrity?
I wonder if I ever thanked you for the sacrifices
you made to let me have the very best?
And for the simple things like laughter, smiles
and times we shared?
If I have forgotten to show you gratitude enough
for all the things you did,
I am thanking you now and I am hoping you knew all along,
how much you meant to me.
Daddy, I will always remember your smile,
your caring heart and warm embrace.
I will remember you being there for us
through good and bad times,
good health and sickness, no matter what!
I will always remember you Daddy,
because there will never be another one
To replace you in our hearts,
and share the love we will always have for you.

Tammy

Tonya Bethel

A Note From Daddy's Little Princess...

Daddy, I'm not sure if they make them like you anymore.
You're a Real Man, cut from a fine cloth.
You're the most unselfish person
that I've been blessed to have known.
You've always been humble
and have taught me to be that way too.
You never looked for praises
and you were never one to boast,
you just went on quietly working hard
for those you loved the most.
You've always been a firm foundation
through all our storms of life,
a sturdy hand to hold in times of stress and strife.
A prayer warrior you were,
never ashamed to call on Jesus' name.
You taught me to BELIEVE, and never give up.
Your faith was beyond measure,
and you taught me just how to trust.
You taught me about FAVOR and reminded me
that Kingdom kids will never go without.
Your jovial spirit and genuine concern
have blessed me in ways too many to count.
Your love was unconditional, and a pure one it was.
I pray to God that I can one day be
as GREAT as you were.

Tonya

Amari Bethel

Bumble to Bee

Daddy, although my years with you were very short (being 16),
there is no one in this world who could ever replace you.
You were the one family member with
whom the majority of my life was spent.
Everywhere you went-I went,
and everywhere you sent-I went.
We were inseparable.
Many did not know that you and I shared a lot of qualities;
whether it was looks, athletics, education, humor
or my favorites-love and happiness.
You were known as Bumble for your athletics
so I made use of your name.
Bumble came from Bumble Bee
because of the speed, strength,
and stinging impact that you used to change people's lives.
Many people know me as Amari Bee.
I branded myself with this title in honor of you,
because you were someone who I could only wish or imagine to be.
I was glad to have you sting my life.

Love, your Bee

Amari

Bibliography

Baxter, R. (1961). "The Savoy Liturgy," in Liturgies of the Western Church (Bard Thompson, ed. ed.). New York: William Collins Publishers.

Collins English Dictionary - Complete & Unabridged 10th Edition. (n.d.).

D. A. Carson. (2002). Worship By The Book. Zondervan.

Eerdman's Bible Dictionary. (n.d.).

Gaddy, G. W. (1992). The Gift of Worship. Nashville: Broadman.

Graham, E. B. (n.d.).

Holman's Illustrated Bible Dictionary . (n.d.).

Holy Bible, New International Version®. (Copyright © 1973, 1978, 1984, 2011).

by Biblica, Inc.® Used by permission. All rights reserved worldwide.

Larsen, B. (n.d.). Luke, p. 59.

Munroe, D. M. (2004). author. Rediscovering The Kingdom. Nassau, Bahamas: Destiny Image Publishers, Inc.

Parent Life. (July 1998, p. 44).

Rines, G. E. ((1920).). "Robinson, Edward (scholar)". . Encyclopedia Americana.

Robinson, H. G. (n.d.).

Spurgeon, C. H. (1870, June 26). A Good Soldier of Jesus Christ.

Strong's Concordance. (n.d.).

The English Bible. (n.d.).

The English Bible. (n.d.).

Webster's New World Dictionary . (n.d.).

Wikipedia. (n.d.). Frazier, Joe.

Wikipedia. (n.d.). JFK.

Wikipedia, the free encyclopedia. (n.d.).

"Empowering Women To Become Focused Agents of Change"

Focused Woman International, founded by Mark's wife Cyprianna in December 2008, is an all encompassing network of professional women determined to encourage, strengthen, define, and refine women to strategically impact their world of influence. This non-profit organization concentrates on providing opportunities for women to utilize their gifts, experiences, and professional skills to enhance the lives of other women.

FWI is founded on Christian principles and is driven by the desire to fulfill a Kingdom lifestyle on earth. The organization is mandated and committed to ensuring that future generations of professionals display the highest level of ethical and Godly standards that transform lives.

FOCUSED WOMAN INTERNATIONAL
P.O. Box EE-17894
Nassau, Bahamas
Tel: 242-364-7718
Emails: info@focusedwoman.com
focusedwomaninternational@gmail.com
www.focusedwoman.com

Worship God Again

Enter His Presence
Like It's Your First Time

Dr. Mark A. Bethel

37484588R10062

Made in the USA
Middletown, DE
27 February 2019